The AIM PROCESS

A Systematic, Stepwise Procedure for Improving the Actionability of Marketing Research

Paul Conner

The AIM Process:

A Systematic, Stepwise Procedure for
Improving the Actionability of Marketing Research
Paul Conner
PC CRS LLC Publishing

Published by PC CRS LLC Publishing, St. Louis, MO
Copyright ©2014
All rights reserved.

Cover and Interior design: www.DavisCreative.com

Paul Conner
The AIM Process: A Systematic, Stepwise Procedure for Improving the Actionability of Marketing Research

ISBN: 978-0-9916295-0-3

*This book is dedicated
to the wisdom conveyed by
legendary UCLA basketball coach
John Wooden when he said,
"Play fast, but don't hurry."*

"Too often data is chosen for analysis because a vendor or boss tells you it is important rather than [supporting] a decision originating with the original research question to be solved. Arguably, nowhere is this currently more true than the pre-occupation with twitter analytics; chosen because it's free and easy to get to, yet representative of less than 8% of the population and severely lacking in signal quality."

— Tom H.C. Anderson in The Future of Market Research.
http://www.tomhcanderson.com/2014/02/26/the-future-of-market-research/.

TABLE OF CONTENTS

FOREWORD

The marketing research and insights industry has seen tremendous change in the last several years and the pace is only quickening. Social media, mobile devices, the Internet and other forms of technology have given researchers a broader set of tools to use and, perhaps more importantly, greater amounts of data. At the same time, research is expected to be delivered faster and cheaper — yet with the same, if not better, quality.

In this context, it's easy to take our eye off the goal of delivering high-quality research that serves its intended purpose: supporting, marketing and business decisions. All too often research is conducted just as a gut-check or to justify an already-completed business action. This lack of clarity or direction can lead to poor outcomes. Or, worse yet, can lead to research being abandoned or not acted upon if the results are not what were expected or if they failed to support marketing decisions. These situations cannot be tolerated. If the insights provided are not actionable, the research department stands a good chance of becoming irrelevant.

The good news is, with the tools and technology currently available, marketing researchers have a real opportunity to help their clients and companies substantially improve the understanding of their business issues and develop solutions to these problems. But the key is to ensure that a systematic procedure is in place before the research is conducted, so that the research is actionable and thus of value to the organization.

The AIM Process

The AIM Process, by Paul Conner, is an excellent example of a simple, clear and logical process to establish a pathway to actionable research. Paul's disciplined, step-by-step instructions address the common challenges of market research and give researchers a guide to ensure that the research they conduct ultimately meets the needs of their clients and businesses.

Steve Quirk
President and Publisher
Quirk's Marketing Research Review

HELLO FROM PAUL CONNER

Hello! I'm a Marketing Researcher[1]. As such, and as you likely expect, I have great interest in conducting highly effective marketing research.

The purpose of this book is to describe a way in which Marketing Researchers and Marketing Research Users can work more effectively to conduct marketing research that accomplishes its primary purpose—supporting marketing decisions and actions.

'Conducting more effective marketing research' implies that it can be improved. Indeed it can. From my experience, a primary problem with marketing research is that the way it's traditionally designed and conducted results in relatively poor actionability. In other words, traditional marketing research practices—particularly practices related to *requesting* marketing research studies—underachieve in supporting marketing decisions and actions. Therefore, if the way we conduct marketing research leaves something to be desired, we need to change the process—in two words, improve it.

That's what **The AIM Process** is all about. By the way, as you'll see, **AIM** stands for **A**pplications, **I**nformation, and **M**ethods, the order of which is critical.

In this book, I...

- Further describe the primary, fundamental problem I see with marketing research today.
- Describe the distinct components and systematic, stepwise procedure for conducting marketing research that address this problem.

---

1 Throughout this book I capitalize certain words like this because they hold prominent meaning for The AIM Process.

The rationale for The AIM Process is not new. Most Marketing Researchers and Marketing Research Users believe in the reasoning behind it. The problem is that most don't use a disciplined procedure that supports the rationale. Hopefully, by understanding and adopting The AIM Process, those days are over. Improved actionability and marketing success is just around the corner.

CHAPTER 1

A FUNDAMENTAL PROBLEM WITH MARKETING RESEARCH

A fundamental problem with marketing research lies in a disconnect between its primary purpose and the procedure by which it's traditionally conceived, designed, and conducted. This disconnect shares much with the seahorse in the following story.

Once upon a time a seahorse gathered his coins and cantered out to find his fortune. Before he traveled very far, he met an eel who asked him where he was going. "To find my fortune," beamed the seahorse. "You're in luck," said the eel. "For one of your coins, you can have this flipper and you'll get there twice as fast." The seahorse gladly paid the eel his money, put on the flipper, and slithered off at twice the speed. Soon he came upon a sponge who asked him where he was going. "To find my fortune," he repeated. "You're in luck," said the sponge. "For a small fee, you can have this jet scooter and you'll get there five times as fast." The seahorse ecstatically paid the sponge, hopped on the scooter, and zoomed off five times faster than before. Soon he met a shark who asked him where he was going. "To find my fortune," he exclaimed. "You're in luck," said the shark. And pointing to his open mouth, he said, "For the rest of your money, you can take this shortcut where you'll find it right away." The seahorse deposited the rest of his coins and swam into the interior of the shark, never to be heard from again. The sad moral of this story is…**if you don't know where you're going, you'll probably end up someplace else!**

The seahorse certainly had a goal—fortune. But was the seahorse's fortune clearly and operationally defined? Furthermore, and more importantly, did the seahorse have a detailed plan for obtaining it? Clearly not.

To understand this fundamental marketing research problem—i.e., its purpose-process disconnect—we need to clarify marketing research's fundamental purpose.

The AIM Process assumes the following about the fundamental purpose of marketing research.

Marketing research exists to support certain decisions and actions that intend to achieve certain outcomes for certain products and services among certain types of people.

Key to this statement of purpose is that **marketing research is an applied discipline**. It exists to be used. It exists to support decisions and actions. Further distinguishing its purpose, marketing research is fundamentally *not* an academic, information-only discipline. Yes, providing information is a necessary component of marketing research, but information itself is *not* its sufficient or defining characteristic.

Some might disagree—most likely Marketing Research Users—saying to Marketing Researchers, "Just give me the information; I'll decide what to do with it." Tom H.C. Anderson, leader of the Next Gen Market Research discussion group on LinkedIn, says this: "Too often data is chosen for analysis because a vendor or boss tells you it is important rather than [supporting] a decision originating with the original research question to be solved. Arguably, nowhere is this currently more true than the pre-occupation with twitter analytics; chosen because it's free and easy to get to, yet representative of less than 8% of the population and severely lacking in signal quality."

Requests like these from Marketing Research Users have more to do with 'who does what' than 'what gets done.' The point is that whoever is charged with using marketing research (i.e., making decisions or taking action from its information), its primary purpose is not effectively fulfilled without decision or action support.

To further clarify this purpose, I claim that "decisions and actions" are collectively the key components in marketing research's fundamental purpose. You'll see later that I collectively call decisions and actions "Applications" (and capitalize that term because of its importance to The AIM Process). If marketing research doesn't support decisions and actions (i.e., Applications), it isn't doing its job. It's flawed and needs to be improved (or in some cases not even conducted).

Accepting this applied purpose of marketing research, its fundamental problem is that the way it's typically designed and conducted does not effectively deliver its intended decision support. Too often at the end of a marketing research study, represented by the final report, Marketing Research Users say things like…

- "This is great information, but what do I do with it?"
- Referring to a key statistic in the results, "Is 24% a good number?[2]"
- "I understand that the study was designed to help me choose a target for my product, but what is it saying about what I should charge for it? Can you please look at the results again and advise me regarding this?"
- "I need to understand better what this is saying about my non-customers. Why didn't we survey them?"
- "This is telling me that 35% of people aware of my brand have negative feelings about it. Where are those negative feelings coming from and how do I change them?"

---

2 This quote comes directly from a client meeting in which a top executive from the client company, who had not been involved in the research before this meeting, asked this question.

Like our friend the seahorse, each of these comments, which have been paraphrased from real world examples, come from people who did not get what they wanted or needed from a marketing research study. Why? And what could they have done to prevent it?

The answers to these questions can have many foci; but all point toward the same thing—a flaw in the procedure. More specifically, the answers likely point to a flaw that diverted it from the fundamental purpose of the study—supporting a certain Application or Applications (i.e., decisions or actions).

To provide evidence for this process flaw, I challenge you. Take a close look at the marketing research studies you're currently conducting, have conducted, or have at least been privy to. About these studies, ask, "What is or was the purpose of the study?" Answer it in your head or write it down. If you can't think of any particular studies, see if you can find a written proposal or report and look at the "objectives" or "purpose" section (if there even is one). As you examine your answer, does the purpose contain any verbiage about what decisions or actions are or were to be made on the basis of the study? My guess is that if I examined your examples, very few would.

Here are examples of what you might find. These have been adapted from actual marketing research proposals or reports:

- The purpose of this study was to (1) measure consumer affinity and willingness to pay for specific features of the product overall and to (2) compare overall appeal and preference for two product models. The study's key objectives were to (a) understand which features of the product are most appealing; (b) measure willingness to pay for specific attributes; and (c) understand the impact of price vs. features on product selection.

- Our objective is to understand consumer attitudes toward shopping for XYZ products in discount stores and to measure the impact of environmental changes with these stores.

- We are interested in measuring the differences in shoppers' perceptions and behavior between open kiosks and walled stores for electronic products in a typical mall.

- XYZ desires to understand the broader context of trends related to shopping for frozen vs. non-frozen desserts and what influences shoppability preferences by demographic and psychographic consumer profiles. Also, XYZ desires to understand drivers and barriers to purchasing frozen and non-frozen desserts at key retailers.

Common to all of these is the omission of clear statements of decisions and actions that the marketing research studies intended to support.

If the fundamental purpose of marketing research is to support marketing decisions and actions, shouldn't every marketing research study proposal and report have a clear understanding and statement of what those decisions and actions are? And shouldn't every element of the design and execution of the marketing research study track logically to those decisions and actions? And shouldn't the first statement from someone who is requesting a marketing research study proposal contain something about the decisions and actions that they need to make on the basis of it? The answer to each of these questions is—you guessed it—yes! However, in actual practice the answer is—unfortunately—no.

Addressing the last question above, how DO Marketing Research Users typically ask for marketing research studies? Here are some examples of how I've been asked:

- "Hey Paul, I need some research to see how people like all the components of our new service. Can you write me up something on that?"

- "Hey Paul, we need some focus groups next week to see what people think of some names for our product. Can you set those up for me?"

- Hey Paul, this weekend we need some research to find out if people are aware of our advertising campaign or not and we need to find out who is and who isn't. I know it's Thursday, but can you please get that done so that we can report to our CEO on Tuesday?

These may be a bit exaggerated, but they're not far from the truth in several respects. At least they reflect different areas of flaws in how marketing research studies are requested.

- Marketing research requests are often made very quickly, without being thought out very well.

- Similarly, marketing research is often needed very quickly, without time to think things out very well.

- Marketing research requesters—ultimately Marketing Research Users—often ask just for techniques.

- Marketing research requesters—ultimately Marketing Research Users—often ask just for information.

- Marketing research requests typically do not include the thoughts of all those who will be involved in the ultimate decisions and actions.

- Marketing research requests seldom clarify the decisions or actions that are to be made on the basis of the research.

Of these flaws, the last is most critical and most represents the fundamental problem with marketing research that The AIM Process addresses—not basing the design and execution of a marketing research study on its primary purpose, supporting marketing decisions and action. By taking an Applications > Information > Methods sequential approach—that is, if we take better "AIM"—marketing decisions and actions will by default be better supported and the money spent on the AIM-guided marketing research study will not be wasted.

**SOME ADVICE ON SHOPPER RESEARCH
FROM ENGAGE'S SHOPPER MARKETING BLOG**

"Don't spend any money on research until you know what you want to know. …It's quite common to hear that a whole load of work has been done and nothing has been learnt. …Most often though the reason for this is because the questions asked are low value."

Tony Desforges, Shopper Marketing Blog, Feb 6, 2013

http://engageconsultants.wordpress.com/2013/02/06/is-shopper-research-the-only-option/?goback=%2Egde_1806202_member_211872196

**TRANSLATION:
QUESTIONS WITH LOW VALUE
DON'T SPECIFICALLY ADDRESS APPLICATIONS!**

Summary

1. Marketing research is inherently an applied discipline. It exists to support marketing decisions and actions. If it does not do this, it's not fulfilling its purpose.

2. A fundamental problem with marketing research is a purpose-process disconnect. Marketing research studies are typically not requested, designed, and conducted to fulfill marketing research's essential purpose—supporting marketing decisions and actions.

3. The primary reason for this purpose-process flaw is that decisions and actions (i.e., Applications) do not lead and sustain marketing research requests, designs, executions, and reports.

4. As you'll see, The AIM Process forces Applications to lead the process, following an Applications, Information, and Methods sequence, but always keeping Applications as the focus.

CHAPTER 2

THE ANATOMY OF A DECISION

In the previous chapter I suggested that both the fundamental purpose and the critical flaw of conducting marketing research studies centers on decisions and actions. Supporting them is the purpose of marketing research, but clarifying them so that they guide the design and execution of studies typically falls short.

Since decisions are key, it's helpful to describe what I call the Anatomy of a Decision. In doing this, I begin to define the components of The AIM Process, which are elaborated in Chapter 3. You'll see that the components of The AIM Process are parts of virtually any kind of decision we make, marketing or otherwise.

Structurally, all decisions are basically the same. We're faced with a **Situation** in which a **Decision** has to be made or an **Action** has to be taken to achieve a certain **Outcome** for a certain **Object or Event (Product)** for a specific **Person or People (Target)**. Sometimes clear **Options** exist, sometimes they do not. To make that decision or take that action, we need **Information**. The information we need depends upon our **Criteria** for making that decision or taking that action.

Some—probably most—of our everyday decisions do not require a great deal of thought about every component. However, most, if not all, decisions proceed through this process.

Here is one example of how a familiar non-marketing decision maps against these components:

Voting

Situation	Every four years our country holds a Presidential election that presents us the opportunity to...
Decision/Action	...decide for whom to vote...
Object (Product)	...for President...
Outcome	...to make this a better place to live...
People (Target)	...for the people that live in this country.
Options	Democratic, Republican, Independent, or other candidate.
Criteria	(One particular person's criteria might be to...) Vote for the candidate that is against capital punishment, is in favor of improving education spending, instills the most confidence, is most honest, and has the strongest civil rights policies.
Information	(If this person were researching to support his/her vote, he/she would collect the following information about the candidates): Where does each stand on capital punishment? On education spending? On civil rights? How honest is each? How much confidence does each instill?

What Marketing Research Users do in their jobs is structurally no different. Here is an example of a typical decision that Marketing Research Users have to make, in this case involving cable television service.

Pricing

Situation	People tell us that they disconnect their cable service because it costs too much. Therefore, we have to…
Decision/Action	…decide what to charge for digital cable television service…
Outcome	…to optimize retention…
Product	…of our digital cable television service…
Target	…among our current digital cable customers.
Options	Although we have a sense of the range of rates to charge, no particular monthly rates are under consideration.
Criteria	We will charge a rate that minimizes service cancellation and that provides acceptable levels of profit.
Information	What percentages of our current digital cable customers will cancel their service at different monthly rates? At any monthly rate along the scale, how much profit will we make?

These fundamental "decision anatomy" examples set up The AIM Process components that are presented in the next Chapter.

Summary

1. Again, supporting decisions is the reason why we conduct marketing research. Therefore, decisions must be effectively represented and sustained to guide the design and execution of any study.

2. Structurally, all decisions are basically the same. They contain Situations, Decisions to be made, Options, Criteria, Objects or Products, People or Targets, and intended Outcomes.

3. These anatomical components make up The AIM Process.

CHAPTER 3

THE COMPONENTS OF THE AIM PROCESS

I think that few would disagree with the fundamental problem of marketing research laid out in Chapter 1. But some would be unfulfilled saying, "Yes, of course marketing research is designed to help marketers make marketing decisions. We believe this and we practice it. Now tell me something I don't know!" Starting with this Chapter, I hope to. At least I hope to define, and later will systematize, things you know but may not practice with great discipline. I start with the components of The AIM Process.

In order to effectively use The AIM Process to improve the actionability of your marketing research, you need to be familiar with the following, some of which are no-brainers, others of which may be implicitly understood, but need explicit clarification, particularly regarding their importance to The Process:

- Marketing Research Users
- Marketing Researchers
- The Situation
- Applications, which are made up of Decisions & Actions, Decision Options, Products & Services, Targets, and Outcomes
- Applications Criteria
- Information Objectives
- Methods
- The AIM Form

Marketing Research Users

Marketing Research Users are individuals who have some or complete responsibility for making decisions or taking actions (i.e., using the research) when the research is complete. They're most often the people who request marketing research studies. Their positions in companies are widely varied, much due to the size and structure of the company; however, Marketing Research Users are typically managers, directors, and VPs (or higher in smaller companies) of marketing or sales functions. As will be emphasized later, typical execution of under-actionable marketing research studies falls short of involving all key Marketing Research Users.

Marketing Researchers

Marketing Researchers are individuals who design, conduct, and report the results of marketing research studies to support the Applications sought by Marketing Research Users. Their positions in companies are typically in research, intelligence, or insights departments.

The Situation

The Situation describes the events that led to a need for a marketing research study, more specifically the need to make or take specific marketing decisions or actions. The Situation is a vital component of The AIM Process because writing it enhances understanding and development of a study's Applications and Information Objectives.

Using its AIM Form section (described in detail later in this Chapter), here is an example of the Situation for a particular study (with CLIENT masked for confidentiality):

1. SITUATION What events led to a need for this research?	CLIENT is a national provider of PRODUCT to young females (primarily 3-18 years old) who are passionate about ACTIVITY regardless of expertise. CLIENT is currently initiating brand strategy work to guide sales of its PRODUCT. Critical to this brand strategy work is the need to deeply understand CLIENT's current and potential buyer segments not only in terms of their sizes, demographics, and purchasing profiles, but also in terms of their "personas" (i.e., their attitudes, personalities, lifestyles, etc.) and purchase decision dynamics (how and why they buy what they buy). Understanding their customers in these ways will help CLIENT executives make a variety of marketing decisions, including, for each of their various lines of PRODUCT, who to target, what messages and images to convey, and how to convey these messages and images in marketing materials (e.g., catalogs and websites). To gain this understanding, CLIENT has asked PC Research to submit a research proposal.

Notice that the Situation is written almost like a story, including a description of the "characters," a brief history, and a description of the "plot" (i.e., problem). In addition, it begins to set up the Applications and Information Objectives for the study.

Applications

Perhaps the signature component of The AIM Process is what I call a study's Applications. Generally, Applications are what the Marketing Research Users need to do with the results of a marketing research study. More specifically, Applications statements include the Decisions & Actions, Outcomes, Products & Services, Targets, and Options to be supported by a particular marketing research study. Each of these are important (in fact, required except for Options) subcomponents of Applications.

Decisions & Actions. Decisions & Actions are the Decisions to be made or Actions to be taken on the basis of a particular marketing research study. "Decide what messages to communicate in our advertising campaign," or "decide what price to charge for our product," or "decide who to target for our product" are all examples of Decisions & Actions. (A more specific list of potential decisions is presented on p.30.)

Decision/Action Options. The only non-required component of an Application, Decision/Action Options are alternative Decisions/Actions being considered. For example, if an Application's Decision is to decide which advertising campaign to launch, its Options may be Campaign A, Campaign B, or Campaign C. Decision/Action Options are not required Application components because not every Decision/Action has pre-determined Options. Deciding who to target for a product may not have specific people being considered until the data are analyzed.

Products or Services. Since the ultimate goal of almost all marketing is to sell a product or service, Applications must identify the product or service being sold. Products or Services, then, are what are ultimately being sold. For example, the Application may be to decide what advertising campaign to launch for the new Ford Mustang, a particular ball point pen, or for donations to the American Heart Association.

Outcomes. Not only do Applications pertain to particular Products or Services, but they intend to achieve certain Outcomes. Outcomes are the behavioral, attitudinal, or financial results to be accomplished by the Decisions/Actions. Outcomes refer to results such as optimizing sales, optimizing share, or optimizing visits.

Targets. Finally, it's important to identify Targets, defined as the specific people for whom the Outcomes are to be achieved. This will obviously direct sampling and analysis during the research execution. Even if deciding who to target is one of the Decisions/Actions, it's necessary to identify at least a general Target to guide the research process.

These subcomponents combine to form an entire Application statement. All components are included, Options when relevant. Examples of complete Applications statements are as follows, positioned within the proper area of The AIM Form (again, a formal description of which will follow).

2. APPLICATIONS	2. APPLICATIONS	2. APPLICATIONS
What decisions/actions need to be made/taken to achieve what outcome for what products/services among whom?	What decisions/actions need to be made/taken to achieve what outcome for what products/services among whom?	What decisions/actions need to be made/taken to achieve what outcome for what products/services among whom?

With the help of this research, CLIENT executives will decide…
• Who to target;
• What personality characteristics to emphasize; and
• What to charge…
…to optimize volume sales of Pre-Historic, CLIENT'S new fragrance, among men aged 35-49.
	With the help of this research, CLIENT executives will decide…
	• What Campaign to choose (A, B, or C);
	• What refinements, if any, to make to it before launch; and specifically…
	• Whether to use red or green in the logo…
	…to optimize share of our brand of car insurance among non-users.
		With the help of this research, CLIENT executives will decide…
		• How to position our restaurant in terms of…
		  • Meal occasions
		  • Food type
		  • Brand personality
		  • General price levels
		…to average $20,000 per month in gross meal revenue among residents in the 11111 zip code.

Applications Criteria

Without question the most difficult and at the same time most important component of The AIM Process is Applications Criteria. Applications Criteria are defined as the rules or guidelines upon which the Decisions/Actions will be made. In essence, Applications Criteria represent how you'll make the Decisions or take the Actions that represent the purpose of the research. If deciding what to charge for your product, what are your criteria? Overall gross revenues that result? Overall gross profit? The most positive perceptions of quality? Or perhaps some combination? These are tough questions to answer because often you just don't know and you figure you'll decide that once you collect and analyze all the data. However, if you don't have at least some idea of your decision criteria, how will you know what information to collect?

In Chapter 4 I'll give specific pointers about how to develop and write Applications Criteria. For now, I present examples of what they might look like within The AIM Form. Please notice that Applications Criteria can (and should) be quite detailed.

2. APPLICATIONS What decisions/actions need to be made/taken to achieve what outcome for what products/services among whom?	3. APPLICATIONS CRITERIA What are the rules or guidelines upon which the decisions/actions will be made/taken?
With the help of this research, CLIENT executives will decide… • What Campaign to choose (A, B, or C); • What refinements, if any, to make to it before launch; and specifically… • Whether to use red or green in the logo… …to optimize share of our brand of car insurance among non-users.	• The chosen Campaign will be that which leads to the greatest degree of associating our brand with quality, activating confidence in our brand, and the highest purchase interest for our brand in competitive buying situations. • Refinements will be made to the chosen Campaign in executional areas that run counter to these three objectives: quality, confidence, and purchase interest vis-à-vis the competition. • The color in the logo, either red or green, will be that which best leads to accomplishment of these three objectives: quality, confidence, and purchase interest vis-à-vis the competition. • Where one Campaign does not win across all three of these objectives, the priority will be purchase interest, quality, and confidence. Furthermore, in this instance, the strategic priorities will be re-examined. • Furthermore, these Criteria assume that the chosen Campaign will not produce reactions that run counter to any of our core mission values.

Information Objectives

Information Objectives are defined as the information to be collected and/or derived to support the Applications via their Criteria. Information Objectives are what Marketing Research Users and Marketing Researchers usually start out with and end up with as statements of the purpose of the research. They represent things that those involved with the research want to find out. In some fields they're called "research questions." Some examples are…

- What do our customers like about our product?
- How much are people willing to pay for our product?
- How do teenagers feel about our logo?
- How long are people waiting on the phone to get to customer service?
- What are people saying about us on Twitter and Facebook?

- How many people have seen our new advertising campaign?

- What different types of people are there who are in the market for XYZ?

- From what zip code are we drawing most of our store visits?

Notice that although these are good "Information" questions, they're not statements of what Decisions to make or Actions to take. These two components—Decisions/Actions and Information—are easily and often confused. Often when I ask clients "What are the decisions you need to make or actions you want to take on the basis of this research?," they answer in terms of Information. For example, I might get answers like the following:

- We want to determine whether or not our product is in our target's consideration set and among how many.

- We want to assess how long it takes someone to open the new packaging we developed.

- We want to find out if the music we're using is consistent with our brand image.

These are statements of desired Information, but not statements of Decisions/Actions to make or take. A relatively easy way to test whether a statement is Information or a Decision/Action is to ask of a statement, "Is the answer to this question or statement something that already exists and can be discovered, or is the answer to this question or statement something that does not currently exist and needs to be executed (at some future point in time)." If it already exists and can be discovered, it's likely Information. If it doesn't already exist and has yet to be executed, it's likely a Decision/Action.

Finally regarding Information Objectives, you may have noticed that they will directly follow from Applications Criteria. In other words, the Information you collect or derive in a study should come from the rules or guidelines you establish for making your Decisions or taking your Actions. Returning to the earlier voting example, if your Criteria for voting for a particular candidate reads, "I will vote for the candidate that is against capital punishment, is in favor of improving education spending, instills the most confidence, is most honest, and has the strongest civil rights policies," then in researching the candidates you'll want to collect Information about how they stand on capital punishment, education spending, and capital punishment, and you'll want to assess how honest the candidate is and how confident you feel about him or her. Again, Information Objectives follow directly from your Applications Criteria.

Methods

Methods are the specific techniques (including sampling, data collection, and analysis) that will be used to provide the Information necessary to support the Application(s) via their Criteria. Methods mark the point at which primary responsibility moves from the Marketing Research Users to the Marketing Researchers who use their expertise to develop and guide exactly how the research is conducted.

Investment and Timing

Investment refers to how much the marketing research study will cost as designed. In the request process, Marketing Research Users communicate and decide how much they're willing to spend and Marketing Researchers work with this to communicate specifically how much the study will cost. Obviously at some point the two come together. Timing refers to the amount of time it will take to conduct the marketing research study as designed. Like for the Investment, in the request process Marketing Research Users communicate and decide how much time they have for the research and when certain phases should be completed and Marketing Researchers determine how long various research tasks will take. Again, obviously at some point the two come together.

Regarding responsibilities, it's important to reiterate that although all Marketing Research Users and Marketing Researchers should work together to develop and execute all components and phases of a research study, there should also be clear assignment of responsibility for each of The AIM Process's various components. Generally speaking Marketing Research Users should be primarily responsible for the Situation, Applications, Applications Criteria, and Information Objectives, while Marketing Researchers should be primarily responsible for the Methods. Regarding Investment and Timing, Marketing Research Users should set the parameters, while Marketing Researchers should obtain study costs and provide a reasonable timetable for executing the research.

The AIM Form

The AIM Form was developed for two purposes:

1. To guide execution of The AIM Process.
2. To provide an efficient (one-page front and back) summary of the background, design, and plan for conducting the marketing research study.

Key to The AIM Form is its efficiency. Although more detailed proposals can and should be developed for a study, The AIM Form allows—in fact, requires—all of the critical components of The AIM Process to be neatly developed and documented.

I start with the front page of The AIM Form.[3]

---

3 Blank AIM Forms can be downloaded by going to http://www.theaimprocess.com/the-aim-process-forms.html.

DRAFT OR FINAL – DATE

USER(S): Name – Company / RESEARCHER(S): Name – Company

STUDY TITLE

This worksheet proposes the Situation, Applications, Information, Methods, Investment, and Timing for a requested research project. Once this proposal is refined and approved, it will be implemented as described.

1. SITUATION What events led to a need for this research?			
2. APPLICATIONS What decisions/actions need to be made/taken to achieve what outcome for what products/services among whom?	**3. APPLICATIONS CRITERIA** What are the rules or guidelines upon which the decisions/actions will be made/taken?	**4. INFORMATION OBJECTIVES** What information needs to be collected or derived from whom to support the Applications?

You'll notice that The AIM Form contains areas for content associated with each of the components and more. At the top of Page 1, you see a place to document the Marketing Research Users and Marketing Researchers. In addition, the Draft # and Date for the Draft are recommended to keep track of revisions. Also, a TITLE is recommended that effectively describes the nature or purpose of the study. Following this header content, the Situation, Applications, Applications Criteria, and Information Objectives are delineated and recorded. The Form guides the research developer by describing what each section should address with a question. A helpful feature of Page 1 of The AIM Form is that Applications, Applications Criteria, and Information Objectives are laid out adjacent to each other so that the relevant flow from one to the other can be established and checked. Remember, Applications Criteria must directly address the specific Applications and Information Objectives should directly correspond to the Applications Criteria. If these correspondences are not established, or if they don't make sense, then the actionability of the research can be threatened.

Now for the back page of The AIM Form, Page 2.

DRAFT OR FINAL – DATE

USER(S): Name – Company / RESEARCHER(S): Name – Company

STUDY TITLE

This worksheet proposes the Situation, Applications, Information, Methods, Investment, and Timing for a requested research project. Once this proposal is refined and approved, it will be implemented as described.

5. METHODS How will the research be conducted?	6. INVESTMENT & TIMING How much will the study cost and what is the schedule for its completion?
7. Authorization Proper signatures are required and indicate authorization to conduct this study as described.	Name, Company Date
Paul Conner, PC Research Date	

Page 2 of The AIM Form repeats the header from Page 1 and continues with a relatively large area to document the Methods for the study—how it will be conducted. Again, detailed Methods should appear in a more comprehensive proposal; however, the space provided here is designed to sufficiently allow for a summary of the Methods.

Following the Methods section is the Investment & Timing section, which delineates how much the study will cost and how it will proceed over time, which is often expressed within a table of tasks and estimated completion dates to reflect the schedule for various phases of the study. In the Investment & Timing section it's also important to delineate any payment terms for the study.

Finally, The AIM Form provides space for Authorization—signing and dating the proposal to indicate that the study has been authorized as described on the Form and any other accompanying documents identified on The Form.

To conclude, The AIM Form provides a platform for (1) stimulating development of the key content for a marketing research study that follows The AIM Process; (2) providing an efficient record of the research background and plan; and (3) providing an official way to indicate and record authorization of the study. Examples of completed AIM Forms appear in Chapters 4 and 5.

Summary

1. The AIM Process involves the systematic integration of several key components that include the background (Situation), purpose & objectives (Applications, Applications Criteria, and Information Objectives), methods (Methods), cost (Investment) and timing (Timing).

2. Delineation of content for all components is easily documented on The AIM Form.

CHAPTER 4

THE STEPS IN THE AIM PROCESS

Having identified the components that will be used in The AIM Process, it's time to describe the stepwise procedure itself. The steps in The AIM Process are as follows:

1. Identify and assign Marketing Research Users and Marketing Researchers.

2. Write the Situation.

3. Delineate the Applications.

    - List the Decisions/Actions and for each Decision/Action…

        - Define its Outcome;

        - Define its Product/Service;

        - Define its Target;

        - Define its Options (if they exist).

4. Develop Criteria for each Application.

5. Determine the Information needed based on the Applications via their Criteria.

6. Specify any Methodological Considerations for the research that will guide its design.

7. Clarify the Investment (i.e., budget).

8. Clarify the Timing.

9. Design, propose, and approve the research Methods.

10. Conduct the research.

11. Report the results of the research in a way that addresses its Applications.

I proceed to elaborate how to conduct each step in the Process, using The AIM Form to document a simple (adapted, not real) example of how it works from my experience in the Broadband Services industry.

Step 1.
Identify and assign Marketing Research Users and Marketing Researchers.

Earlier I said "typical execution of under-actionable marketing research studies falls short of involving all key Marketing Research Users." It's critical that this step not be taken lightly. Not only for communications purposes, but also for effective actionability when the research is complete, identifying and involving key individuals responsible for using the research (i.e., those making decisions and taking action based on it) must be done.

When he was at Capital One, James Mendelsohn of CAN Capital may have said it best in a meeting I attended with him several years ago:

"Research is not a spectator sport."

Too many times Marketing Research Users, especially those at higher levels, don't get involved because they rely on the Marketing Researchers and lower-level Marketing Research Users to do their job and they jump in when it's finished. This just doesn't work. If they're not involved in the beginning, they don't understand the Decisions and Actions that the research was originally designed to support. Often, when the research is finally completed perhaps three to six months after it was conceived, they impose their current decision needs on the research, expecting it to support them. With this scenario, more often than not, the research just doesn't comply, and problems arise. Researchers struggle to make the data fit their "decisions du jour," often violating valid use of the research.

I hope you get the point. It's ugly when appropriate Marketing Research Users are not included from Day 1. And, most importantly, it most often leads to less than optimally actionable research. Therefore, The AIM Process says that all Marketing Research Users must be involved and active from the beginning and throughout because, after all, it's they who will be using the research and if they're not represented throughout, they won't be served in the end.

The AIM Form includes a place for recording the Marketing Research Users and Marketing Researchers. It's the very first line of the header, placed there so it follows on every page of the Form. I start our example by assigning Bob Johnson and Tom Merlotti as the Marketing Research Users and me as the Marketing Researcher for the Broadband example I'll be creating.

DRAFT 1 — February 20, 20XX

USER(S): Bob Johnson, Tom Merlotti – National Broadband/ RESEARCHER(S): Paul Conner – PC Research

DIGITAL CABLE CAMPAIGN ASSESSMENT RESEARCH

1. SITUATION What events led to a need for this research?	

On the Form, it may be sufficient to include only the key Market Research Requesters/Users and Market Researchers. However, it's wise to record all potential Marketing Research Users on the Form to keep them involved in the Process and even to require them to specifically approve each step along the way.

Step 2.
Write the Situation.

To bring the following components of The AIM Process into context, it's important to clarify the events that led to a need for the research in the Situation. Situations can take on their own format and content, but I recommend the following:

- Begin by identifying the primary company, relevant products and services, and any other key players and briefly describe key events that created a need for the research.

- Arrive at the main issue being addressed in the research; for example, the need to create a positioning or the need to understand how a new product is received.

- Introduce the nature of the Applications (e.g., targeting, pricing, package design, etc.) as well as the nature of the Information needed to support them.

- Conclude by stating essentially that "research is needed to address this issue."

Here is an example of the Situation for the Digital Cable Campaign Assessment Research written on the Form.

DRAFT 1 — February 20, 20XX

USER(S): Bob Johnson, Tom Merlotti – National Broadband/ RESEARCHER(S): Paul Conner – PC Research

DIGITAL CABLE CAMPAIGN ASSESSMENT RESEARCH

1. SITUATION What events led to a need for this research?	National Broadband is a cable television and Internet services company that operates throughout the United States. Their advertising agency, Giddyup, is developing a new Campaign designed to increase National Broadband's share of TV cable subscribers versus satellite and fiber optics providers as it has decreased over the past year. National Broadband's digital cable TV service has several advantages over its competition—more channels to choose from, higher quality picture, and the best channels in its most popular packages. National Broadband and Giddyup executives have to decide which of these three features to focus on in the Campaign's messages. They have asked PC Research to conduct research to support their decision.	
2. APPLICATIONS What decisions/actions need to be made/taken to achieve what outcome for what products/services among whom?	**3. APPLICATIONS CRITERIA** What are the rules or guidelines upon which the decisions/actions will be made/taken?	**4. INFORMATION OBJECTIVES** What information needs to be collected or derived from whom to support the Applications?

Step 3.
Delineate the Applications.

To review, Applications are the fundamental component of The AIM Process and contain several subcomponents: Decisions/Actions, Decision Options (optional), Products/Services, Targets, and Outcomes. An effective Application statement contains all of these components, except where no Decision Options exist.

Who is responsible for writing the Applications? Technically, since they're charged with acting on the research, Marketing Research Users should develop the Applications. However, this responsibility is seldom acted upon, or even understood, in practice. As I said earlier, most marketing research is conceived at the Information or Methods level, so Marketing Research Users typically don't even think about or communicate exactly what they want to do with the research once it's completed. In fact, it's all too common that when Marketing Researchers ask Marketing Research Users "what decisions do you need to make on the basis of this research?" (the fundamentally essential question), they have trouble articulating them.

Over more than 20 years of working with The AIM Process, I've developed a set of Decisions and Actions that can help Marketing Research Users develop this component. This set, comprised of 30, is presented on the next page. Although this set may not include every possible Decision/Action, or word them in the exact way that you might, it covers most Decision/Actions that a marketing research study will be asked to support. I invite you to use it to guide you in delineating the Decisions and Actions for your research.

	30 COMMON DECISIONS/ACTIONS TO BE SUPPORTED BY MARKETING RESEARCH
1	What do we want this product to do?
2	Should we offer this product or not?
3	Who should we target for this product, including how should we describe the target?
4	What competitive categories and/or products should we target?
5	What competitive brands should we target?
6	How should we design the product in term of its features; content and/or aesthetics and/or operational?
7	If it has different components, how should we bundle the product as an offering?
8	How should we instruct people to consume/use the product?
9	How much should we charge for the product?
10	How should we charge and/or bill for it?
11	What special deals should we use to sell it?
12	How should we design the package of the product to look?
13	How should we design the package of the product to work (e.g., open)?
14	How should we provide service for the product?
15	Where should we sell the product in terms of "channels?"
16	Where should we sell the product within the chosen channels?
17	Where should we sell the product geographically?
18	How should the selling location and product presentation within it be organized/designed?
19	How should the product be distributed to the place of sale?
20	What do we want the target(s) to think about the product ITO its personality, its values, and its functional benefits?
21	How do we want the target(s) to feel when using the product?
22	What should we say about the product to deliver the positioning?
23	How should we say what we say executionally?
24	What cognitions should be leveraged?
25	What experiences should be leveraged?
26	Where should we say what we say in terms of media vehicles?
27	Where should we say what we say geographically?
28	At what points in the path to purchase should we intervene?
29	How should the path to purchase interventions be designed?
30	At what times of week, day, year should we deliver the messages?

Once the Decisions and Actions are chosen, each should be associated with Options (if they exist), Products and Services, Targets, and Outcomes within efficiently written sentences. For example, if you need research to help you decide what to charge for a new cereal among older adults, the Applications statement might read as follows:

"On the basis of this research, we will decide how much to charge (Decision) for a 14 oz. box of Flakes Cereal (Product) among adults 60+ years old (Target) to get them to switch to Flakes Cereal versus their current brand (Outcome)." (Note: No concrete Options exist for this Application).

The reason to include all of these components is to inform various parts of the research design and analysis. Delineating the Decisions informs relevant Information to collect and analyses to perform. Delineating the Product (or Service) seems quite obvious, but it provides the object of study. Delineating the Target informs the sampling process. And delineating the Outcome informs the type of behavior to ask people about or observe in the data collection.

Continuing with The AIM Form for our Digital Cable Campaign Assessment Research, the Applications may be added as follows:

DRAFT 1 — February 20, 20XX

USER(S): Bob Johnson, Tom Merlotti – National Broadband/ RESEARCHER(S): Paul Conner – PC Research

DIGITAL CABLE CAMPAIGN ASSESSMENT RESEARCH

1. SITUATION What events led to a need for this research?	National Broadband is a cable television and Internet services company that operates throughout the United States. Their advertising agency, Giddyup, is developing a new Campaign designed to increase National Broadband's share of TV cable subscribers versus satellite and fiber optics providers as it has decreased over the past year. National Broadband's digital cable TV service has several advantages over its competition—more channels to choose from, higher quality picture, and the best channels in its most popular packages. National Broadband and Giddyup executives have to decide which of these three features to focus on in the Campaign's messages. They have asked PC Research to conduct research to support their decision.		
2. APPLICATIONS What decisions/actions need to be made/taken to achieve what outcome for what products/services among whom?	**3. APPLICATIONS CRITERIA** What are the rules or guidelines upon which the decisions/actions will be made/taken?	**4. INFORMATION OBJECTIVES** What information needs to be collected or derived from whom to support the Applications?	
With the help of this research, NATIONAL BROADBAND executives will decide… • What Campaign to choose (A=more channels, B=quality picture, or C=best packages); and • What refinements, if any, to make to it before it launches… to optimize share of its digital cable subscription versus satellite and fiber optics subscribers.			

Step 4.
Develop Criteria for each Application.

As I said earlier, perhaps the most important part of The AIM Process, but also the most difficult, is developing Criteria for each Application. This step defines the rules and guidelines that will dictate the Decisions and Actions you will make or take in the end.

Criteria are difficult to clarify up-front because you don't always know how you'll make decisions. You can't always anticipate all of the decision factors. Despite this difficulty, in a research project it's critical that you think through the process as best you can because the Criteria dictate the Information that needs to be collected and/or derived. The Information has to address your Criteria. Otherwise, the Decisions and Actions will be based on no or irrelevant Information. Furthermore, you should not collect or derive Information that is not in the Criteria because that will make the research wasteful and more expensive than it needs to be. Finally, for most effective actionability, developing the Criteria should include all relevant Marketing Research Users. Many marketing research studies have been ineffective, or have had to be changed in mid-stream, because a senior executive who was not included early on had a different set of Criteria for making a Decision or taking an Action.

In writing Criteria statements, it's helpful to include some part or form of the Decision or Action in the beginning of the statement. For instance, in our Digital Cable Campaign example, we start the Criteria statement with, 'We will choose the Campaign that...' Then we conclude the statement with the specific Criteria.

To make the Criteria relate to the Applications, a space for Applications Criteria on The AIM Form has been placed right next to the space for the Applications. As such, continuing our example, Applications Criteria appears as follows on The Form:

DRAFT 1 — February 20, 20XX

USER(S): Bob Johnson, Tom Merlotti – National Broadband/ RESEARCHER(S): Paul Conner – PC Research

DIGITAL CABLE CAMPAIGN ASSESSMENT RESEARCH

1. SITUATION What events led to a need for this research?	National Broadband is a cable television and Internet services company that operates throughout the United States. Their advertising agency, Giddyup, is developing a new Campaign designed to increase National Broadband's share of TV cable subscribers versus satellite and fiber optics providers as it has decreased over the past year. National Broadband's digital cable TV service has several advantages over its competition—more channels to choose from, higher quality picture, and the best channels in its most popular packages. National Broadband and Giddyup executives have to decide which of these three features to focus on in the Campaign's messages. They have asked PC Research to conduct research to support their decision.	
2. APPLICATIONS What decisions/actions need to be made/taken to achieve what outcome for what products/services among whom?	**3. APPLICATIONS CRITERIA** What are the rules or guidelines upon which the decisions/actions will be made/taken?	**4. INFORMATION OBJECTIVES** What information needs to be collected or derived from whom to support the Applications?
With the help of this research, NATIONAL BROADBAND executives will decide… • What Campaign to choose (A=more channels, B=quality picture, or C=best packages); and • What refinements, if any, to make to it before it launches… to optimize share of its digital cable subscription versus satellite and fiber optics subscribers.	• Among the target market, the chosen Campaign will be that which leads to the greatest degree interest in switching from their current satellite or fiber optics provider to National Broadband's cable TV service. • Refinements will be made to the chosen Campaign in executional areas that diminish competitive purchase interest. • Furthermore, these Criteria assume that the chosen Campaign will not produce reactions that run counter to any of our National Broadband's core mission values.	

Step 5.
Determine the Information needed
based on the Applications via their Criteria.

Once the Applications and their Criteria are written, the Information Objectives emerge directly, particularly from the Criteria. Following the logic of The Anatomy of a Decision, you only need to collect or derive Information that addresses your Criteria (and Information that allows you to address the Outcome and identify the Target).

In writing the Information Objectives, the following are important:

- To remind you where the Information Objectives are coming from, begin writing the Information Objectives section with the phrase "In order to support the Applications via their Criteria... ."

- Examine the Applications and Applications Criteria sections, looking for aspects that will need measurement. Make sure that Information Objectives include Information you'll need to identify the Target and assess the Outcome. (Note: This is excluded from The Form that follows for simplicity's sake.)

- When the Information section is complete, check to make sure all aspects of the Applications and Applications Criteria are covered.

- Also make sure that each point of Information relates to some aspect of the Applications or Criteria.

On The Form, Information Objectives sit right next to the Applications Criteria for easy transition and checking. In our example, this is what The AIM Form looks like with the Information Objectives section complete.

DRAFT 1 — February 20, 20XX

USER(S): Bob Johnson, Tom Merlotti – National Broadband/ RESEARCHER(S): Paul Conner – PC Research

DIGITAL CABLE CAMPAIGN ASSESSMENT RESEARCH

1. SITUATION What events led to a need for this research?	National Broadband is a cable television and Internet services company that operates throughout the United States. Their advertising agency, Giddyup, is developing a new Campaign designed to increase National Broadband's share of TV cable subscribers versus satellite and fiber optics providers as it has decreased over the past year. National Broadband's digital cable TV service has several advantages over its competition—more channels to choose from, higher quality picture, and the best channels in its most popular packages. National Broadband and Giddyup executives have to decide which of these three features to focus on in the Campaign's messages. They have asked PC Research to conduct research to support their decision.	
2. APPLICATIONS What decisions/actions need to be made/taken to achieve what outcome for what products/services among whom?	**3. APPLICATIONS CRITERIA** What are the rules or guidelines upon which the decisions/actions will be made/taken?	**4. INFORMATION OBJECTIVES** What information needs to be collected or derived from whom to support the Applications?
With the help of this research, NATIONAL BROADBAND executives will decide… • What Campaign to choose (A=more channels, B=quality picture, or C=best packages); and • What refinements, if any, to make to it before it launches… to optimize share of its digital cable subscription versus satellite and fiber optics subscribers.	• Among the target market, the chosen Campaign will be that which leads to the greatest degree interest in switching from their current satellite or fiber optics provider to National Broadband's cable TV service. • Refinements will be made to the chosen Campaign in executional areas that diminish competitive purchase interest. • Furthermore, these Criteria assume that the chosen Campaign will not produce reactions that run counter to any of our National Broadband's core mission values.	In order to support the Applications via their Criteria, the following information will be collected and/or derived among people who currently subscribe to satellite or fiber optics television service: 1. How much does each Campaign lead to interest in switching from their current provider's TV service to National Broadband's digital cable TV service? 2. What aspects of each Campaign lead to increased and decreased interest in switching? 3. Accounting for a variety of reactions to each Campaign (e.g., message communication, brand equity conveyed, etc.), what reactions are consistent and inconsistent with National Broadband's core mission values and which ones?

Steps 6-10.
Methodological considerations
through conducting the research:

6. Specify any Methodological Considerations for the research that will guide its design.

7. Clarify the Investment.

8. Clarify the Timing.

9. Design, propose, and approve the research Methods.

10. Conduct the research.

The next five steps in The AIM Process are important, but not as critical to improving the actionability of marketing research by using a better request process. These five steps have more to do with designing appropriate research techniques than they do with making sure the correct Applications are defined and the Information collected or derived fits the Applications via their Criteria.

In determining Methodological Considerations, issues of sampling and data collection should be explored. For example, Marketing Researchers should ask and Marketing Research Users should answer questions such as...

- With what degree of precision and confidence do we want to generalize the results to the target population? (This impacts sampling strategies.)

- Do we want to actually see and hear the target give their answers? (This impacts data collection techniques.)

Clarifying the Investment and Timing are also issues that affect the research design. Different Methods will be proposed given different amounts of money to spend and different time constraints.

Designing, proposing, and approving the research Methods turns a research request process (which I am really dealing with in this book) into a proposal process. At this point, understanding all of the Applications, Applications

Criteria, Information Objectives, Methodological Considerations, Investment, and Timing, the Market Researchers design the techniques (sampling, data collection, and analysis) that will be used to collect and analyze the data to support the Applications via their Criteria.

I show the second page of The AIM Form here, but the Methods are simply "considerations" and the Investment and Timing are more tentative than when the Applications, Applications Criteria, and Information Objectives are clarified and agreed upon and the Methods are detailed in the formal proposal. Again, this book deals more with using The AIM Process for "actionability preparation" than for research Methods design and execution.

DRAFT OR FINAL – DATE

USER(S): Name – Company / RESEARCHER(S): Name – Company

STUDY TITLE

This worksheet proposes the Situation, Applications, Information, Methods, Investment, and Timing for a requested research project. Once this proposal is refined and approved, it will be implemented as described.

5. METHODS How will the research be conducted?	6. INVESTMENT & TIMING How much will the study cost and what is the schedule for its completion?
At this point, the Methods are being designed and will be detailed in the final proposal. Methodological considerations are as follows: • The study is to be conducted so that results generalize to the target population, including subgroups of interest, with a minimum precision of ± 6% at the 90% level of confidence. • The Campaigns will be represented in rough video format. Data collection must be able to accommodate rough video. • As regional variations can be produced, reads for each of National Broadband's five regions are required. • Block groups will be provided that represent National Broadband's operational footprints, but sample will not be provided. • Qualitative comments from surveys are acceptable for diagnostics; live focus groups or IDIs are not necessary.	**Investment:** The total cost for this research has yet to be determined. However, a range of $30,000 to $40,000 is tentatively set. **Timetable:** The timetable for the research has not been determined; however, the final report is needed by April 30, 20XX.
7. AUTHORIZATION Proper signatures are required and indicate authorization to conduct this study as described.	Name, Company Date	Paul Conner, PC Research Date

Conducting the research simply means collecting and analyzing the data as designed. If carried out as designed, the research will support the Applications via their Criteria.

This leads us to the last step in The AIM Process.

Step 11.
Report the results of the research
in a way that addresses its Applications.

As stated in the beginning of this book, marketing research exists to support specific Decisions and Actions. If, when the research is complete, it does not accomplish this goal, it's ineffective. Sometimes a marketing research study has the *potential* to accomplish this goal (i.e., the necessary Information was collected or derived), but does not because the Information collected is not organized and reported in a way that clearly addresses the Applications.

The AIM Process directs structure for reports, presentations, and executive summaries to accomplish the goal of actionability. Instead of simply "spitting out" pages and pages of tables, charts, or narratives, any Information should be strategically structured to address the study's Applications through their Criteria and Information Objectives. (Since Criteria and Information Objectives go hand-in-hand, either can be used.) Reports should organize and present results in "Decision-Based" sections rather than sections that relate to topics of Information. For example, in the study we've been designing, we see two major sections of results:

- Results related to which Campaign to choose.
- Results related to how to refine the chosen Campaign.

In a report, data are organized in charts, tables, graphs, or figures to address or answer each of these questions.

Many companies desire and use "one-pagers."[4] These are short executive summaries—preferably one-page long—that communicate the bottom-line, key information needed for decisions to be made or actions to be taken. The AIM Process is conducive to such executive summaries. Included in decision-based executive summaries are the following:

- A restatement of the Applications along with their Criteria.
- Suggestions or recommendations that directly address the Applications.
- Conclusions that pertain to each Criteria or area of Information.
- Data support that contains the results that led to the conclusions.

Using our example, and providing fictitious data that may have resulted from the study, such an executive summary in a one-page format might look like that on the following page for the primary Application of this study—deciding which Campaign to choose: A, B, or C. Similar tables can be constructed for each Application that was established for a particular study.

---

4 Depending on the number of Applications, a one-pager may not be possible. What is more important is the structure of the summary rather than its length.

APPLICATIONS AND THEIR CRITERIA	SUGGESTED ACTION	CONCLUSIONS	DATA SUPPORT		
APPLICATION: What Campaign should National Broadband choose to optimize their share of digital cable subscription versus satellite and fiber optics subscribers? (Campaign A, B, or C) CRITERIA: Choose the Campaign that leads to greatest interest in switching to NB and that does not produce reactions that run counter to any of National Broadband's core mission values.	CHOOSE CAMPAIGN C – BEST PACKAGES	Campaign C led to the greatest interest in switching for both satellite and fiber optics subscribers. Campaign C was most consistent with NB's core mission values of integrity and customer service.	**Interest in Switching to NB (Avg. 5-pt Scale)**	**SAT**	**FB**
			CAMPAIGN A	3.82	3.46
			CAMPAIGN B	4.07	3.68
			CAMPAIGN C	4.22	3.96
			SAT = Satellite Customers; FB = Fiber Optics Customers		
			% Saying Campaign Conveyed INTEGRITY	**SAT**	**FB**
			CAMPAIGN A	35%	42%
			CAMPAIGN B	26%	38%
			CAMPAIGN C	54%	60%
			SAT = Satellite Customers; FB = Fiber Optics Customers		
			% Saying Campaign Conveyed CUSTOMER SERVICE	**SAT**	**FB**
			CAMPAIGN A	35%	42%
			CAMPAIGN B	26%	38%
			CAMPAIGN C	54%	60%
			SAT = Satellite Customers; FB = Fiber Optics Customers		

CHAPTER 5

CASE STUDIES

The previous chapters, which described the components and steps in The AIM Process, provided relatively simple and deliberate examples. Although the components and steps are the same for any marketing research study, they can get more detailed and nuanced depending on the study being designed. Because of this, I present 3 examples of how The AIM Process was used to guide the design and execution of actual studies. Here I present the actual pre-proposal AIM Forms along with brief commentary on how each study was conducted and what decisions and actions were taken on the basis of the results—actions which obviously addressed the Applications for which each study was conducted.

The three case studies have been altered only in terms of company names and product categories. The issues and content remain as they were in the actual execution of each study. These cases involve:

- Acme Ball Point Pens
- Lakeville Resort
- Brown Can Soda

FINAL 2 – April 2, XXXX

USER(S): James Smith – Acme Corporation / RESEARCHER(S): Paul Conner - PC Research

ACME BALL POINT PEN EMOTIONAL DRIVER RESEARCH

1. SITUATION What events led to a need for this research?	Acme Corporation (Acme) markets a full line of writing devices, particularly for business writing. Of their product offerings, ball point pens have been targeted for this project. Obviously seeing the importance of emotions in consumer decisions and behavior, Acme executives have become interested in understanding what emotions most drive people to purchase a ball point pen and the degree to which the Acme brand triggers these driving emotions vs. its strongest competitor Nifty. To explore these categorical and brand-associated emotions, and ultimately to support their efforts to develop new communications (e.g., packaging, advertising, and PR) for their ball point pens, Acme has asked PC Research to provide a research proposal.

2. APPLICATIONS	3. APPLICATIONS CRITERIA	4. INFORMATION OBJECTIVES
What decisions/actions need to be made/taken to achieve what outcome for what products/services among whom?	What are the rules or guidelines upon which the decisions/actions will be made/taken?	What information needs to be collected or derived from whom to support the Applications?
With this research, Acme executives intend to develop/refine their communications plans (which include plans for packaging, communications, advertising, and public relations) for their ball point pens by... • Deciding the specific emotions to target within these plans and (optionally)... •Deciding how to activate these specific emotions... ...all in order to optimize sales of these devices (particularly vs. Nifty) among business people that either own or are considering owning a ball point pen. [Note: These Applications are considered developmental in nature, thus do not require precise sampling or quantitative verification of results.]	Specific emotions to target for activation will be those that... • Are positive in nature and... • Sufficiently drive the target to purchase a ball point pen and... • Are or can be strongly associated with or drive purchase/purchase interest of Acme ball point pens... particularly in relation to Nifty. Furthermore, they will be emotions that are or can be consistent with (and certainly not inconsistent with) Acme's overall competitive brand positioning. (On the flip side, specific emotions to target for de-activation will be those that are negative in nature and do just the opposite as described above in relation to Nifty.) If deciding how to activate the targeted emotions is sought, ways to activate these emotions will come from understanding the experiences (i.e., things that people see, hear, or otherwise experience) and/or cognitions (i.e., knowledge, beliefs, opinions, attitudes, etc.) that activate these emotions in the target.	In order to support these Applications via their Criteria, this research will collect and/or derive relevant qualitative "experiEmotive" information (a.k.a. experiEmotives) among business people that either own or are considering owning a ball point pen. experiEmotives are the experiences, cognitions, and emotions associated with and/or driving various concepts, brands, objects, or actions. This research will collect and/or derive experiEmotive's related to... • Business writing in general; • Ball point pens in general; • Purchasing ball point pens; • Acme and Nifty in general; • Acme and Nifty ball point pens; • Purchasing Acme and Nifty ball point pens.

Because the Applications for this study were developmental in nature, 10 targeted consumers were recruited to participate in a 2-day series of qualitative psychodramatic "action interviews" during which key emotions (and their experiential and cognitive triggers) related to using and buying ball point pens from Acme and Nifty were explored.

The research identified 13 potential Emotional Themes for Acme to consider. The Emotional Themes delineated positive emotions to augment, negative emotions to mitigate, and their experiential and cognitive triggers. One of these Emotional Themes—pens from an Accomplished Professional—was recommended and used to compete against Nifty. This positioning called for targeted pen users to feel successful and superior.

Moving on to Lakeville Resorts, the next pages show The AIM Form.

FINAL 1 — June 22, XXXX

USER(S): Jo Anne Johnson – Lakeville Resort / RESEARCHER(S): Paul Conner - PC Research

LAKEVILLE LAND DEVELOPMENT RESEARCH

| **1. SITUATION**
What events led to a need for this research? | Lakeville is a private residential and recreational living community located approximately 50 miles west of Anytown consisting of some 1,200 homes and 90+ lakes on approximately 7,400 acres of land. At the present time, Lakeville is looking toward its next stage of development, which will consist of adding property and amenities to approximately 1,000 to 2,000 acres of land. Lakeville executives are seeking market/consumer research to help them decide what to do with this land to increase property ownership by acquiring new property owners (POs) without inordinately losing current ones. |

2. APPLICATIONS What decisions/actions need to be made/taken to achieve what outcome for what products/services among whom?	3. APPLICATIONS CRITERIA What are the rules or guidelines upon which the decisions/actions will be made/taken?	4. INFORMATION OBJECTIVES What information needs to be collected or derived from whom to support the Applications?
For the 1,000 to 2,000 acres of new land at Lakeville, decide… 1. What to do with the land (i.e., what types of amenities and/or property to build on it); 2. Who to target for marketing Lakeville with the new amenities and/or property (in terms of demographics, geodemographics, cognitions, and/or emotions); 3. How to position Lakeville to the chosen target(s) with the new amenities and/or property; 4. How to communicate the chosen positioning to the chosen target(s) (e.g., what specific messages to convey, what executional elements to employ, and/or what media vehicles to use)… all in order to optimize the number of prospective POs (Prospects) who find Lakeville attractive enough to purchase property there (without inordinately disenchanting current POs [Currents] toward selling their property).	Pertaining to Application #1, develop the land in ways that optimize Prospects' interest in purchasing property at Lakeville; are acceptable to Lakeville Management; do not inordinately violate Lakeville's desired culture or cultural themes; and do not inordinately disenchant Currents toward selling their property. Pertaining to Application #2, target people who offer sufficient revenue potential and whose "hot buttons"* for the land development are acceptable to Lakeville Management; do not inordinately violate Lakeville's desired culture or cultural themes; and do not inordinately disenchant Currents toward selling their property. Pertaining to Applications #3 and #4, position Lakeville to the chosen target(s) and communicate the chosen positioning in ways that are consistent with their "hot buttons" for the land development; are consistent with their media habits and preferences; are acceptable to Lakeville Management; do not inordinately violate Lakeville's desired culture or cultural themes; and do not inordinately disenchant Currents toward selling their property. *Hot buttons will involve experiences, cognitions, and emotions/feelings that lead to positive purchase interest in Lakeville property.	In order to support the Applications (and achieve their Outcomes) via their Criteria, the following Information needs to be collected and/or derived among Prospects: 1. Their awareness of Lakeville. 2. Their overall cognitions (beliefs, attitudes, impressions, etc.) of Lakeville. 3. Their overall feelings toward Lakeville. 4. Their interest in buying new property at Lakeville overall and given certain plans (and property prices) to develop the new land. 5. Derived estimates of how much revenue will be generated by different plans among different targets. 6. Cognitions and emotions associated with certain plans to develop the new land and, related to this, derived estimates of the degree to which certain cognitions and emotions "drive" purchase interest (i.e., "hot buttons"). 7. Their demographics and geodemographics. 8. Their media habits and preferences. In addition, the following information needs to be collected among Currents: 9. Their interest in keeping or selling their property at Lakeville given certain plans to develop the new land.

To help target respondents, Prizm analyses were conducted among Lakeville's current Property Owners and interested non-Property Owners. Next, telephone interviews were conducted to learn about their general awareness and interests. Next, 10 in-depth relaxed-mind-state interviews were conducted to understand deep-seated emotional drivers of property purchase. Finally, an on-line survey was designed to help Lakeville assess current Property Owners' reactions to the land development recommendations.

The key insight was that Lakeville needed to tap into the theme of "Reliving Childhood through Nature." All land development ideas needed to be consistent with how "the child" in all of us finds emotional value in nature.

This research helped Lakeville fine tune its overall positioning and use that fine-tuned positioning to guide its choices and designs for developing its recently purchased land. In addition, the positioning led to changes in Lakeville's internal corporate culture statements and operating procedures.

Moving on to Brown Can Soda, the next pages show The AIM Form.

FINAL 2 — April 2, 20XX

USER(S): James Smith – Acme Corporation / RESEARCHER(S): Paul Conner - PC Research

BROWN CAN SODA'S PURCHASE DYNAMICS AND COMMUNICATIONS DEVELOPMENT RESEARCH

| 1. SITUATION
What events led to a need for this research? | Brown Can Soda (BCS) is one of Cosmopolitan Soda's U.S.'s (CSUS) innovative brands, offering premium soda in a can. Despite many rational, functional benefits of premium soda in a can vs. a bottle (e.g., it's less expensive per unit, the special can packaging keeps the soda fresher for longer, the larger can minimizes having to open several bottles), a stigma remains about "the can" vs. "the bottle," which limits sales. CSUS executives are currently interested in developing a concept statement and communications for BCS. To do this, they need to understand the "purchase dynamics" for the premium canned soda category and for BCS in particular. What experiences, cognitions, and emotions drive premium soda consumers toward and away from purchasing canned vs. bottled soda and BCS vs. its competitors? To address this issue, CSUS has asked PC Research to develop a research proposal. |

2. APPLICATIONS What decisions/actions need to be made/taken to achieve what outcome for what products/services among whom?	3. APPLICATIONS CRITERIA What are the rules or guidelines upon which the decisions/actions will be made/taken?	4. INFORMATION OBJECTIVES What information needs to be collected or derived from whom to support the Applications?
With the help of this research, CSUS will… Develop a concept statement and communications directives for Brown Can Soda (BCS). These will include statements of… • Whom to target; • What emotions to augment and/or mitigate; • How to augment or mitigate those emotions via canned soda's, BCS's, and/or bottled soda's… • Product features (and their "rational, functional" benefits/disadvantages) and/or… • Specific cognitions. These "decisions" ultimately intend to optimize sales of BCS among premium soda consumers (specific definition TBD). (The components of these Applications are based on evidence that behavior is driven by emotions triggered by tangible "experiences" [e.g., product features] and "cognitions" [e.g., knowledge, thoughts, beliefs, values, etc.].).	CSUS will target people who already believe, or are open to believing, that premium canned soda (including BCS) is worthy of purchase and have already purchased it or express a strong intent to purchase it (in addition to, or instead of, premium bottled soda). (We'll abbreviate this positive purchase [intent] PPI.) Target characteristics will primarily include beliefs they have, and the emotions they trigger, leading to this PPI. Emotions to augment and/or mitigate will be those that most impact PPI – likely augmenting positive emotions that increase PPI and mitigating negative emotions that decrease PPI. Product features (and their rational/functional benefits/disadvantages) and cognitions will be those that activate, or are at least associated with, the emotions that impact PPI.	In order to support the Application(s) for this research, the following Information will be collected and/or derived among premium soda consumers (specific definition TBD): 1. What is their current purchase behavior and/or purchase intent for premium canned soda, BCS, and its primary competitors (Goodie and Curtis) vs. bottled soda? 2. For what occasions do they purchase or show positive intent to purchase premium canned soda, BCS, and its primary competitors vs. bottled soda? 3. Including those that are "implicit" (i.e., automatic, unconscious, and/or guarded), what specific emotions "drive" positive and negative purchase (intent) for premium canned soda, BCS, and its competitors vs. bottled soda? 4. Including those that are implicit, what cognitions (i.e., knowledge, thoughts, beliefs, values, self-perceptions, etc.) activate the emotions referred to in #3? 5. What tangible "experiences" (including product features) and their rational, functional benefits activate the emotions and cognitions referred to in #3 and #4 above. 6. In summary, what feature-cognition-emotion augmentations or mitigations (including associated rational/functional benefits/disadvantages) most enhance positive purchase (intent) of BCS?

In this study, Brown Can Soda and its competitors were subjected to quantitative implicit and explicit priming exercises using well-founded social psychology priming techniques. These exercises revealed discrete emotions that were associated with and impacted purchase of the various brands, obviously including Brown Can Soda.

Following up these quantitative exercises, individuals who showed emotional profiles of strategic interest were recruited to participate in a series of qualitative one-on-one interviews. These interviews provided a deeper understanding of the nature and causes of the implicit and explicit feelings associated with Brown Can Soda—particularly the ones that most impacted its purchase vs. competitors.

Eighteen different emotional themes emerged for consideration, from focusing on feeling enlightened and self-actualized to feeling smart and in control. The chosen positioning was a hybrid that included feeling enlightened, self-actualized, and somewhat redeemed (from the stigma of being a canned soda drinker) by being a Brown Can Soda drinker.

CHAPTER 6

SUMMARY AND SUGGESTIONS

Much too often, marketing research studies fail. They don't accomplish their ultimate purpose of supporting marketing decisions. When this happens, the primary reason most likely lies within one or all of the following:

- A lack of sensitivity to the fundamental components and steps involved in formal decision-making;

- A lack of patience to follow those steps;

- A lack of diligence in gathering and including the key decision makers throughout the entire marketing research process; or

- A lack of caring among all decision makers (particularly those at higher levels) to stay engaged in the marketing research study, particularly at key decision points along the way.

The AIM Process is a systematic, stepwise procedure for addressing these challenges and ultimately improving the actionability of marketing research studies. The key to The AIM Process is taking the time to clearly state Applications (Decisions/Actions, Outcomes, Products/Services, Targets, Options), Applications Criteria, and Information Objectives before designing and conducting marketing research studies and including and engaging the proper people in that process.

| DESIGN | EXECUTION | DESIGN | EXECUTION |

TYPICAL time spent
conducting stages of
marketing research studies.
(Shape area = relative amount)

AIM PROCESS time spent
conducting stages of
marketing research studies.
(Shape area = relative amount)

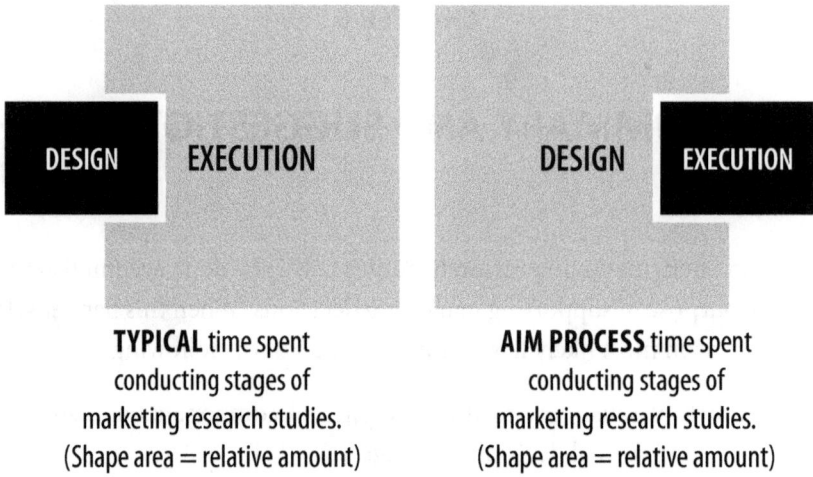

Regarding "taking the time," the simple graphic at left illustrates a fundamental organic problem in the typical research request process. Relatively little time is devoted to designing the marketing research study compared to much more time devoted to executing it.

Contrast this graphic with how The AIM Process calls for the allocation of time and you'll see that the same amount of time is involved, but it's redistributed between designing and executing the marketing research study.[5] The thinking is that if more time is spent effectively designing studies up front, less time will be needed to execute them at the back end because corrections for incompletely or inaccurately conceived Applications and the Information Objectives that result from them will not have to be made. Furthermore, in using The AIM Process, studies may not have to be completely scrapped because they don't sufficiently support their intended Applications.

Hopefully The AIM Process as described here is logical and clear enough to pursue in practice. As logical and clear as it may be, there are challenges to be aware of.

---

5 In many cases, these time representations are figurative rather than literal. Obviously, some studies—for example, longitudinal studies that extend over months or even years—need to take longer to execute than to design. The point is that relatively more time needs to be devoted to designing marketing research studies up front than is typically taken.

1. Do not rush through the process. Requesting marketing research should not be a 10-15 minute "hallway conversation."

2. Include all people who have some knowledge or investment in the Applications. This especially includes senior executives. Otherwise the Information you collect or derive may be insufficient or irrelevant.

3. Decisions/Actions are not the same as Information. They're often confused. Make sure your Decisions/Actions are not statements of Information.

4. Even though different types of people are responsible for different parts of The Process, it's clear that all can and should work together along the way. It's important to realize, however, that ultimate responsibility for stating Applications, Criteria, and Information Objectives lies with Market Research Users, and ultimate responsibility for designing and conducting the research lies with Marketing Researchers.

It's too bad that the seahorse in Chapter 1 couldn't read. Or maybe if the seahorse could read, it may be too bad that he didn't have access to The AIM Process before setting out to find his fortune.

The AIM Process helps Marketing Researchers and Marketing Research Users know where they're going so they don't end up someplace else.

FURTHER INFORMATION AND CONTACT

Thank you for your interest in The AIM Process. I sincerely hope that you find it useful in designing and conducting marketing research studies. In addition to this book, I am available for in-person seminars to help you better understand and use The AIM Process.

Related to such studies, I hope you will consider working with Emotive Analytics (http://www.emotiveanalytics.com) to understand the emotional dynamics related to purchasing your or your clients' products and services. Recent research in neuroscience and psychology has shown the importance of emotions (and other affective phenomena) in directing all human decisions and behavior, including consumer decisions and behavior. Furthermore, such emotional dynamics operate in large part subconsciously, therefore need to be assessed using non-traditional "implicit" research techniques. Emotive Analytics specializes in those techniques.

Whether for help with The AIM Process or help with emotional dynamics research, I look forward to hearing from you. Here is how you can contact me and see more about my work:

Paul Conner | paul@theaimprocess.com | paul@emotiveanalytics.com

Also visit **The Consumer and Shopper Insights Applied Educational Alliance** website www.appliededucationalalliance for more opportunities to learn how to understand and apply emotional dynamics of consumer behavior.

APPENDIX

Forms, Worksheets, and Exercises

The following pages provide the following for you to use in designing your marketing research studies via The AIM Process:

- The first and second (front and back) pages of a complete AIM Form.

- Separate sections of the AIM form for you to more easily work with individually in constructing your research design.

Obviously, there is only one copy of each page in this book. To download free copies of blank worksheets, go to http://www.theaimprocess.com/the-aim-process-forms.html.

DRAFT # – Date

USER(S): Name(s), Company (ies) / RESEARCHER(S): Name(s), Company (ies)

NAME OF STUDY

This worksheet proposes the Situation, Applications, Information, Methods, Investment, and Timing for a requested research project. Once this proposal is refined and approved, it will be implemented as described.

1. SITUATION What events led to a need for this research?	

2. APPLICATIONS What decisions/actions need to be made/taken to achieve what outcome for what products/services among whom?	**3. CRITERIA** What are the rules or guidelines upon which the decisions/actions will be made/taken?	**4. INFORMATION** What information needs to be collected or derived from whom to support the Applications?

DRAFT # – Date

USER(S): Name(s), Company (ies) / RESEARCHER(S): Name(s), Company (ies)

NAME OF STUDY

This worksheet proposes the Situation, Applications, Information, Methods, Investment, and Timing for a requested research project. Once this proposal is refined and approved, it will be implemented as described.

5. METHODS How will the research be conducted?		6. INVESTMENT & TIMING How much will the study cost and what is the schedule for its completion?
7. AUTHORIZATION Proper signatures are required and indicate authorization to conduct this study as described.	Name, Company Date	Paul Conner, PC Research Date

DRAFT # – Date
USER(S): Name(s), Company (ies) / RESEARCHER(S): Name(s), Company (ies)

NAME OF STUDY

This worksheet proposes the Situation, Applications, Information, Methods, Investment, and Timing for a requested research project. Once this proposal is refined and approved, it will be implemented as described.

1. SITUATION
What events led to a need for this research?

DRAFT # – Date

USER(S): Name(s), Company (ies) / RESEARCHER(S): Name(s), Company (ies)

NAME OF STUDY

This worksheet proposes the Situation, Applications, Information, Methods, Investment, and Timing for a requested research project. Once this proposal is refined and approved, it will be implemented as described.

2. APPLICATIONS What decisions/actions need to be made/taken to achieve what outcome for what products/services among whom?

DRAFT # – Date

USER(S): Name(s), Company (ies) / RESEARCHER(S): Name(s), Company (ies)

NAME OF STUDY

This worksheet proposes the Situation, Applications, Information, Methods, Investment, and Timing for a requested research project. Once this proposal is refined and approved, it will be implemented as described.

3. CRITERIA
What are the rules or guidelines upon which the decisions/actions will be made/taken?

DRAFT # – Date

USER(S): Name(s), Company (ies) / RESEARCHER(S): Name(s), Company (ies)

NAME OF STUDY

This worksheet proposes the Situation, Applications, Information, Methods, Investment, and Timing for a requested research project. Once this proposal is refined and approved, it will be implemented as described.

4. INFORMATION
What information needs to be collected or derived from whom to support the Applications?

DRAFT # – Date

USER(S): Name(s), Company (ies) / RESEARCHER(S): Name(s), Company (ies)

NAME OF STUDY

This worksheet proposes the Situation, Applications, Information, Methods, Investment, and Timing for a requested research project. Once this proposal is refined and approved, it will be implemented as described.

5. METHODS
How will the research be conducted?

DRAFT # – Date

USER(S): Name(s), Company (ies) / RESEARCHER(S): Name(s), Company (ies)

NAME OF STUDY

This worksheet proposes the Situation, Applications, Information, Methods, Investment, and Timing for a requested research project. Once this proposal is refined and approved, it will be implemented as described.

6. INVESTMENT & TIMING
How much will the study cost and what is the schedule for its completion?

ABOUT THE AUTHOR

Paul Conner has been a consumer/marketing researcher since 1982 serving a variety of businesses and working for all company types—agency, client, and supplier. In 2004 he founded Emotive Analytics (originally experiEmotive analytics), a consumer research firm devoted to assessing the emotional dynamics of consumer behavior. Mr. Conner's works and thinking have been published in Quirk's, QRCA Views, and Marketing News as cover stories and articles on topics such as consumer emotions, behavioral economics, and research design. Furthermore, he has spoken at AMA, QRCA, IFT, Path to Purchase Institute, Design & Emotion Society, and CTAM conferences and events.

www.ingramcontent.com/pod-product-compliance
Lightning Source LLC
Chambersburg PA
CBHW071241200326
41521CB00009B/1572